Tammy Does **Boston**

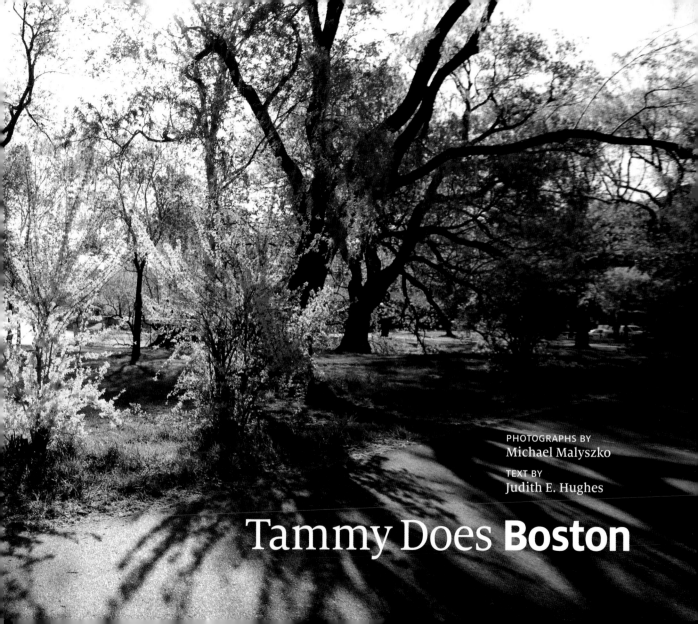

PHOTOGRAPHS BY
Michael Malyszko

TEXT BY
Judith E. Hughes

Tammy Does **Boston**

Library of Congress Control Number: 2009942918

ISBN: 978-0-615-31806-6

Printed in China.

Tammy Tours
90 South Street
Boston, MA 02111 USA

tammydoesboston.com

Tammy, rescued as a young puppy in West Virginia, came into our lives thanks to a wonderful network of shelters and foster care agents who work tirelessly to find loving homes for unwanted pets. Five percent of our profits from this book will be donated to further this important work.

To Rita (1991-2007)
Thanks for showing me the ropes.
Tammy

My name is **Tammy**. Aren't I pretty?

If you've got four days, I'll show you my city.

In Boston it's best to start with our **history**.
Follow the red bricks or paint. It's no mystery...

Freedom Trail in front of the Old State House

Old North Church/Copp's Hill

To find a good spot to stop and to sit
And see the old **steeple**,
where lanterns were lit...

That sent riders off to warn of Red Coats.
But only **Revere** got a history note.

Paul Revere Statue

Then over and up Bunker Hill's monument
To catch a fine view and then take a jaunt...

Bunker Hill Monument

Down to the docks to see
"Old Ironsides"...

The U.S.S. Constitution

That great battleship
and our local pride.

This **old meeting hall** is now where we come

To see our new folks

become full citizens...

Faneuil Hall

Or step just outside on a fine summer day

And make some new friends watching **jugglers** play.

Juggler At Quincy Market

Curley's Statue

Then zip across North Street and see if you fit through
The tall, narrow legs of Mayor Curley's statue!

Now, let's go find a nice **place to dine**
Where we'll sit outdoors if the weather is fine.

The South End

Let's start our parks' day with an **Esplanade** run.
Next stop, Beacon Hill, where Boston begun...

The Esplanade

By building it's streets on twisty cow paths.
Acorn's the one that's the most photographed.

Beacon Hill

Nearby in the Garden,
our **Swan Boats** just glide

'Round the pond, pedal-powered.
Do take a ride!

The Public Garden

Make Way For Ducklings Statue

Most kids like to sit on these brass ducklings' backs.
Myself, I preferred to pretend to be Quack.

Boston Common

The big park next door is known as **the Common**
With expanses of grass my friends and I roll on.

New State House

Near the top, our "new" **state house** (really quite old)
Has a beautiful dome that's leafed with real gold!

Our **Fenway**'s a park, but only in name.
I watched the pros warming up for a game...

Fenway Park

Then trotted on off to a spot that's more risky:
The right field foul pole named for Johnny Pesky.

The Pesky Pole

The CITGO Sign

This big **neon sign** was once dim and blighted.

But with world champs near by,
they keep it well lighted.

Then let's end our day back where we began...

In front of the **Hatch Shell** hearing a band.

The Hatch Shell

Our museum day
should start with a treat.

Fried dough is yummy,
but awfully sweet!

Fried Dough

So to quench my big thirst,
I took a big slug

Of delicious cold milk
from this **super-sized jug**.

Near the Children's Museum

The city's **aquarium** keeps seals in a pool,
Where they swim upside down.
Isn't that cool?

The New England Aquarium

At the **Science Museum**, the fake lightning bolts

Looked pretty scary, but delivered no jolts.

The Museum of Science

On our way to some others, let's take time to shop.
Haymarket's food prices will make your jaw drop.

Haymarket

Newbury Street

And so will the prices on **Newbury Street**
(But for quite different reasons) on clothes that are chic.

Do you think it's art—what this Indian's doing—
Guarding the door to our **Fine Arts museum**?

The Museum of Fine Arts

On our way back downtown, we'll zag and then zig
Past a **fountain** they've built where they dug the Big Dig.

The Rose F. Kennedy Greenway

The Institute of Contemporary Art

When our newest **museum** kept me outside,
I made my own piece from a bone of rawhide...

Which maybe I'll sell or put on display
Down in hip SoWa on the next first Friday.

First Fridays in SOWA

On this our last day, let's start with a dip.
Bright and early, I gave **the pond** guards the slip!

The Frog Pond

Well, that felt so good, I went for another
In a pool by a church some call the "**Mother**".

The Christian Science Center

Next, how 'bout a sail?
Community Boating

Costs just a few bucks
to get you out floating.

Sailing on the Charles

Chinatown

Time to refuel! By the **Chinatown Gate**

There's a park to take in the take-out I ate.

Nearby at South Station, look what I found—
Me in an ad. What a talented hound!

South Station

If it's April, this must be Boston's **big race.**
I stopped for a drink to sustain my fine pace.

Heartbreak Hill at the Boston Marathon

In August our city's **North End** hosts big feasts...
You might see me lead the parade through the streets...

North End Festival - Parade

And then take a turn to pin a few bucks
On the saint's plaster **statue** to bring me good luck.

North End Festival - Statue

Now that it's dark, we can see a free flick.
The hotel on **Rowe's Wharf** has got just the trick.

Movie night on Rowe's Wharf

The Zakim Bridge

We've seen quite a bit and it's time that we part
Beneath our **new bridge**, a real work of art!

Some say that the cables are spread like a sail.
Others say that they're like the leaves of a book.

I could care less which opinion prevails.
I think it's gorgeous however your look.

Afterword

Tammy came into our lives in the fall of 2000, brought up from West Virginia via a wonderful network that rescues unwanted mixed breed puppies. We met Tammy at the Northeast Animal Shelter in Salem, Massachusetts just a month and a half after Betty passed away. If you've seen our earlier books (*Betty & Rita Go To Paris,* 1999 and *Betty & Rita, La Dolce Vita,* 2001) you know she had some pretty big paws to fill!

And fill them she did. Bright-eyed and bushy-tailed, Tammy jumped into our arms and hearts the minute we met her. Having just lost her best friend, Rita was a bit slower to warm up. Although their friendship deepened in a matter of weeks and proved steadfast to the end, Rita most decidedly declined to be part of another book. So *Tammy Does Boston* became a one-dog adventure.

Of course, creating this book took a village—actually a city, and we'd like to give a shout out to all those who took us to and sometimes into places, who modeled for us, and who assisted us in production (pre- and post-).

Let's start with those who opened doors: Lynne Paget, owner of the Boston Swanboats; Deirdre Coyle & Meg Vallaincourt for getting us into Fenway Park; Carl Zukroff & Mike Alexander of the Museum of Science; Jennifer Standley of the Museum of Fine Arts; Susan Barrow-Williams & Marcin Kunicki of Community Boating; Peter Shields of the Boston Harbor Hotel; Guy Martignetti of the Feast of St. Anthony; the store personnel at DKNY on Newbury Street; and a wink and a nod to those at the USS Constitution who let us past the ropes...

To our models: Oriana Anholt, Arlo Brandt, Maeve Malyszko, Martha Wheeler and the lad "pedaling" the Swanboat; Tammy's dear departed friends Chelsea & Gunther; all those tired runners at Heartbreak Hill; and the gentleman minding the saint's statue...

To a few who defy categorization: Bob & Louisa Miller for the ride in the swell convertible and Sean Mahoney for putting Tammy in an ad...

To our interns and assistants: Ashley Tilton, Anna Walsh, Jill Candlish, Mariel Feldman, Tina Gianos and Matt Yee...

To our book designer, Shawn Hazen, and our publishing consultant, Amanda Freymann...

Thank you all from the bottom of our hearts.

About the Authors

Michael Malyszko, the photographer, and Judith Hughes, the author, run a successful commercial photography studio and split their time between a loft in Boston and a cottage in Gloucester. They are the authors of *Betty & Rita Go To Paris* and *Betty & Rita, La Dolce Vita,* published by Chronicle Books in 1999 and 2001, respectively.